MW00461303

Unworthy But Called

Joe Joe Dawson

Table of Contents

Introduction

Unworthy but Called! There are literally billions of people on planet Earth that truly feel unworthy to live out the calling that God has placed on their lives. Somewhere along the journey of life, numerous people have believed a lie that made them feel unworthy to go after their God-given dreams and calling.

Research says that between 90-95% of people will never accomplish their goals, dreams or walk in their God-given calling. There is an identity problem that is going on today, but this same problem has been going on since the beginning of time. When we fully and truly understand who we are in God, then and only then, will we be able to completely walk in all that He has called us to do.

True happiness comes from being in the very center of God's perfect will for your life. Things will not always be perfect but when you know you are in the middle of God's plan, you can get through anything. This book is to help people find their true identity in God. Once you know your true identity then you can say "yes" to the calling that He has placed upon you.

God has an amazing vision for your life and He does not want you weighed down any longer by feelings of insecurity and inadequacy. My prayer is that this book will be a tool God uses to renew your mind and deliver you completely from every lie that has made you feel unworthy or disqualified from the amazing future He has for you.

It is my earnest hope that this message, straight from your heavenly Father's heart to yours, will equip you to forever leave feelings of unworthiness behind and be transformed by the confident knowledge that you are a deeply cherished child of God called to do great exploits for His Kingdom!

Chapter 1:
Your Identity

I love the feeling I get when everything is lining up perfectly with the call that God has placed on my life. We all love the seasons where we are so on fire for God, our passion is blazing for Him and it seems as though nothing can stop the God-ordained purpose and plan for our lives. You know what I'm talking about!

But life doesn't always feel that way. I also happen to know what it feels like to feel so low that you don't know where to turn. It feels as if you've hit rock-bottom and then gone even lower. There are times in life where you don't know who to talk to, where to begin, or how to turn it around. You may even have moments when you wonder, "Will things ever get better?"

We all have good seasons as well as difficult seasons, but do you know what's different about God's calling on your life in both situations? Absolutely nothing. Your situation and current circumstances have absolutely no bearing on the calling that God has on your life. The tests, trials and tribulations you go through do not alter or negate God's original purpose and intent for your life.

Difficult seasons are a part of God's process to develop and prepare you for the promises that He has given you and the future He has planned for you. They are meant to help mold and shape you into the person that God has called you to be. You must understand your calling is from God and the gifts He has given you are activated, no matter what.

Romans 11:29 says, "For the gifts and the calling of God are irrevocable." Another version says, "The gifts and calling of God are under full warranty." We must always remember that God never sends anyone to this Earth without a calling or purpose. The enemy will always fight you to make you feel unworthy to step up and step out into all God has called you to do. You must always remember that before you were born, you were called!

Jeremiah 1:5-9 says, "Then the word of the Lord came to me, saying, "Before I formed you in the womb I knew you; before you were born I sanctified you; I ordained you a prophet to the nations. Then I said, "Lord God, Behold, I cannot speak, for I am a youth." But the Lord said to me: "Do not say, 'I am a youth,' For you shall go to all whom I send you, and whatever I command you, you shall speak. Do not be afraid of their faces, for I am with you to deliver you," says the LORD."

Before, we were ever even formed in our mother's womb, we were created in the heart and mind of God. God, the good Father has placed a mighty, purposeful, powerful calling on each of us. The gift mix that God has given you will sustain you and help move you forward into the destiny God has for you.

No one is born worthless. Hard situations, circumstances, trials, tests and things people or the enemy have spoken over you may have made you feel unworthy, but God, the ultimate Father, has deemed you worthy and has placed His stamp of approval on you by giving you a special calling and specific gifts.

God's call on your life can be identified by the natural and spiritual gifts that you may have and will usually be confirmed by prophetic words spoken over you. Whenever the enemy hears a prophetic word from Heaven over someone, he tries to unleash every strategic attack of warfare he can against that person and the calling that God has on their life.

The most powerful thing that you have in your natural body is your mind. If the enemy can control the way you think, he can control everything about you. This is why we must keep a current and fresh personal relationship with Jesus Christ and our minds continually renewed by the Word of God. Daily time with God will help you feel worthy to walk in the calling that He has placed upon you.

If you feel like the enemy has been trying to get you to compromise or walk in confusion, know that you are in good company. Satan even tried to get Jesus to compromise His calling. After Jesus had been baptized by John, the Father spoke life and blessing over Him. Jesus understood the importance of His calling at a greater dimension. Then, to consecrate His walk with God, Jesus went on an extended fast.

Matthew 3:16-17 "When He had been baptized, Jesus came up immediately from the water; and behold, the Heavens were opened to Him, and He saw the Spirit of God descending like a dove and alighting upon Him. And suddenly a voice came from Heaven, saying, "This is My beloved Son, in whom I am well pleased." What a powerful example of the affirmation of the Father toward Jesus, His Son. This was the confirmation that God spoke to Jesus. God called Jesus not just His son, but His beloved Son. Then He went on to say that He was well pleased with Him.

Whenever you are under an open Heaven, you will feel the power and presence of God in a whole new dimension as you experience His glory. Hopefully all of us have had a similar experience of approval and confirmation from Father God. We need to feel the power, presence and glory of God in such a great degree as the Lord speaks words of affirmation over us about our calling and purpose.

Matthew 4:1-3 says, "Then Jesus was led up by the Spirit into the wilderness to be tempted by the devil. And when He had fasted forty days and forty nights, afterward He was hungry. Now when the devil came to Him, he said, "If You are the Son of God, command that these stones become bread."

The very first thing that the devil did was try to get Jesus to question His identity as the Son of God. He questioned Him by saying, "If you are the Son of God...?" The devil was questioning His identity. Did Jesus not already hear that from His Father? Whenever we hear affirmation from God, we must realize that the enemy will try to come in and steal our sense of identity and security in Christ. The enemy wants us to feel unworthy to do what God has called us to do.

The next thing the enemy said was, "Turn these stones into bread." The enemy said this to try to get Jesus' mind off what He was called to do and get Him to focus on carnal things. The enemy could not get Jesus to question His identity, so he tried to get Him to compromise. When you know who you are in Christ, the enemy will always try to make you compromise.

When we relax in our walk with God, the devil will try to whisper confusion into our ears in an attempt to distract us. The enemy will use many of these things to try to pull us away from the heart of the Father. When we are not seeking the Father, spending intimate time with Him on a regular basis, it is easier for the enemy to attack us with feelings of unworthiness about our calling.

Matthew 4:4 says, "But Jesus answered and said, "It is written, 'Man shall not live by bread alone, but by every word that proceeds from the mouth of God." Jesus answered the devil right back with the Word of God. God wants us to follow Jesus' example in dealing with the devil and his lies and temptations. Whenever the devil sends us an invitation to sin or compromise in some way, we can decline every single attempt with the Word of God.

The Bible is the inspired Word of God, and it is full of true prophetic words from Heaven. We have to learn to stand on the Word of God and fight with the prophetic words spoken over our lives. This will enable us to overcome all of the devil's attacks, whether subtle or obvious. When the enemy comes in to try to make you question your identity or calling, quote Scripture and declare the prophecies that have been spoken over you! Declare your calling and fight with the Word of God.

When the devil could not get Jesus to question His identity or compromise, he tried to convince Jesus to harm Himself. Matthew 3:5-6 says, "Then the devil took Him up into the holy city, set Him on the pinnacle of the temple, and said to Him, "If You are the Son of God, throw Yourself down. For it is written: 'He shall give His angels charge over you,' and, 'In their hands they shall bear you up, lest you dash your foot against a stone.'"

The enemy twisted Scripture and misinterpreted the Word to try to manipulate Jesus. Then Jesus fired right back with the Word of God in Matthew 3:7 which says, "Jesus said to him, "It is written again, 'You shall not tempt the Lord your God.'" We must know the Word of God and know how to use Scripture, because the Word is our sword.

Matthew 3:8 says, "Again, the devil took Him up on an exceedingly high mountain and showed Him all the kingdoms of the world and their glory. And he said to Him, "All these things I will give You if You will fall down and worship me." Once again, the devil tried to get Jesus to compromise, but it was no use. Remember, Jesus has all authority in Heaven and on Earth but the devil was still trying to get Him to compromise. If he tried it with Jesus, it is no wonder he tries it with you.

Sometimes in our lives we may not fully see all that God has given to us as His sons and daughters and joint heirs with Jesus Christ. The devil will attempt to take advantage of this to offer us a partial truth that may seem appealing and good. It may even appear to be a shortcut to all that we have been promised in Christ when, in fact, God had so much more for us.

Feeling unworthy may cause us to not want to wait for the right time, but receiving the right thing at the wrong time can be dangerous. Doing so will teach us we have so much more to learn before we are fully prepared to inherit all that God has in store for us.

Matthew 3:10-11 says, "Then Jesus said to him, "Away with you, Satan! For it is written,

'You shall worship the LORD your God, and Him only you shall serve.'" Then the devil left Him, and behold, angels came and ministered to Him." Once again, Jesus fought and overcame the attack with the written Word, then used His authority to rebuke Satan and end the conversation.

Many times, the attacks of the enemy will come right before your biggest breakthrough. The enemy will often try to get your mind off what the Lord has called you to do and try to come in and whisper lies of compromise and deceit to get you to think naturally instead of supernaturally. The calling that God has placed upon you is supernatural so don't let the enemy get you to think naturally about it. We must be wise to the attacks of the enemy that would try to deceive us to prevent us from accomplishing our God-given purpose on Earth.

Chapter 2:
Worthy To Be Counted On

God knows exactly how to position the right people in the right place, at the right time, equipped with the right things. Many times, we may look around at our current situation and think, "I am the least likely person God could use."

You may even look at your surroundings and say, "Everybody else could be used by God at this very moment but me." But you may be the very one that God is about to use. Never count yourself out of being the one that God wants to use to bless others or bring a breakthrough.

I love the story about the young boy who had a few fish and a few loaves of bread. Jesus had just finished teaching and was surrounded by a huge multitude. It was getting late and there was nothing for them to eat. Jesus knew ahead of time this situation was going to happen and He already had it all under control.

John 6:8-9 says, "One of His disciples, Andrew, Simon Peter's brother, said to Him, "There is a lad here who has five barley loaves and two small fish, but what are they among so many?" Sometimes you may look at the gifts that God has given you and think, "Lord there's not much here." But when the multiplying power of God touches your talents and abilities, they will be exponentially increased to become whatever He needs them to be. There is no limit or measure to God nor to what He can do with a fully surrendered life.

The little boy offered up the little bit that he had and Jesus made it more than enough to cover the needs of the multitudes that were before Him. Sometimes you may feel like you don't have a lot to offer the people in your family or your workplace. But when you turn what you have over, and place it in the hands of Jesus, He will multiply it to meet the needs of the people He has called you to impact and bless for the Kingdom of God.

John 6:10-13 says, "Then Jesus said, "Make the people sit down." Now there was much grass in the place. So, the men sat down, in number about five thousand. And Jesus took the loaves, and when He had given thanks He distributed them to the disciples, and the disciples to those sitting down; and likewise of the fish, as much as they wanted. So, when they were filled, He said to His disciples, "Gather up the fragments that remain, so that nothing is lost." Therefore, they gathered them up, and filled twelve baskets with the fragments of the five barley loaves which were left over by those who had eaten."

You see, the multitude numbered 5,000 men, not including the women and children. The little boy wasn't even worthy enough to be counted, but he was the one that the Lord counted on. When the disciples were counting the men, the little boy may have stood up on his tip toes but they may have passed him by. However, when the Lord needed someone, the boy didn't look at the ground and withhold what he had.

The men may have deemed him as unworthy to be counted but God found him worthy to be counted upon. You may have been overlooked on so many occasions in your life but now is the time that you are about to be used by God in mighty ways!

There are times that men and women will overlook you, pass you by and count everybody else but you. However, that's when the eyes of the Lord are especially upon you. God will encourage you to step up and offer what you have in a crucial moment. You may feel like you are unworthy but, my friend, you were called for such a time as this. To all the people that have been overlooked, know that God sees you and He is about to multiply your efforts!

The young boy was unworthy to be counted amongst the men, yet he was the very one God used to deliver the people from their hunger. I believe there are countless people today who are starving spiritually, but God is raising up the outcasts, the overlooked, the rejected, and the misfits who have offered up their fully surrendered lives to meet the needs of those hungry and desperate for Him.

Stop and think about it for a moment. When Peter was restored after his betrayal, Jesus specially commissioned him in John 21:15-17 to, "Feed My sheep." God is raising up the ones who feel unworthy to be counted on because of the lies they have believed or from how others have handled them. He wants them to know they are specially hand-picked by Him and He has an amazing calling and purpose for their lives!

In Jesus' time, the rabbis and priests would pick the young boys that they were going to disciple from a young age. These would be the ones who would eventually take their place as priests and rabbis to fulfill their sacred duties in the temples, tabernacles and synagogues. If you had not been chosen by the time you were 12 years old, you had to take up your father's trade. If you were considered unworthy to be a priest or rabbi, you had to work for your father and fully take on and learn his trade in business.

Remember, when Jesus chose His 12 disciples, they were already in their father's trade. The first four were fishermen and one was a tax collector. When Jesus called His 12, they probably responded something like this, "Well pastor, bishop, priest or rabbi so and so said I was unworthy to be called into the ministry." Jesus probably looked at them and said, "I know they said you were unworthy, but I'm telling you, "you are worthy!" I'm calling you to be my disciple. You are the one that I want!"

Never let man's opinion steer you away from your God-given calling and purpose in life. Others may have told you that you are unworthy. You may even feel like it's too late, or like you have made too many mistakes.

You might even have believed the lie that your little life couldn't possibly make any impact on the multitudes of people and problems in the world. But those are all lies from the pit of hell because God says you are worthy and you are called!

I absolutely love the story of how God called Moses to become a deliverer for His people. Moses had more reasons why he was not the one for the position than anyone in the history of the world. God asked him to go back to a land where the ruler did not like him. He was wanted for murder, and he had family there that didn't really know or care for him.

Also, Moses wasn't a very good communicator. In fact, he stuttered pretty badly. There wasn't a single thing in the natural that would have qualified him to be the one God would use to deliver His people from bondage. Except one thing: he was born and specially called for that exact purpose! Moses even tried to explain to God why he was unworthy to fulfill the assignment that God was calling him to. I know you're probably laughing at Moses right now for arguing with God. But in reality, how many times, by your words, thoughts or actions, have you told God you're unworthy to do what He has called you to do?

Exodus 3:4 says, "So when the LORD saw that he turned aside to look, God called to him from the midst of the bush and said, "Moses, Moses!" Then Moses said "Here I am." The two things that are very important in this passage are the same things that are important for us today. First, God called out to Moses. Second, Moses answered. Whenever God calls out to us and speaks our name, it is important for us to answer with an open heart, a willing mind and say, "God here I am."

The Lord started talking to Moses and sharing His heart with him about His children who were in bondage in Egypt. Many times, God will start to speak to us about people who, by looking at their outward circumstances and situations, feel completely lost and rejected and appear to have lost all hope. But God is always looking for deliverers who will have the true heart of Father God and will give their lives as an answer to what He wants to accomplish in the lives of others. The heart and will of God is created in Heaven but needs someone to manifest them on the Earth. God is always looking for a remnant to bring His plans from Heaven to Earth in order to see the Kingdom of God manifested.

Exodus 3:7-8 says, "And the Lord said: "I have surely seen the oppression of My people who are in Egypt, and have heard their cry because of their taskmasters, for I know their sorrows. So, I have come down to deliver them out of the hand of the Egyptians, and to bring them up from that land to a good and large land, to a land flowing with milk and honey." If you could see the size of the call that God has upon your life, and the importance of that plan, you would no longer allow lies and distractions to side track, confuse or pull you away from it.

Every person has been strategically placed at the right moment in time throughout history. Everything you have gone through, and will go through, in life will be used by God to accomplish His great purposes. Not one thing you've gone through will be wasted. When God gives you a calling, you better take it, my friends! It is your life work and life mission. Don't ever let anyone else, or yourself, talk you out your God-given calling.

Many times, people will be in prayer and cry out "God use me! Use me to touch the nations of the world; use me as a minister, entrepreneur, or business owner!" Then, when the Lord speaks, we tell God why we're unworthy or unqualified to do what He has called us to do. I often laugh at people who try to talk themselves and God out of the very thing they were created to do.

Exodus 3:11 says, "But Moses said to God, "Who am I that I should go to Pharaoh, and that I should bring the children of Israel out of Egypt?" Moses was basically telling God, "I think You got the wrong man for the job." Moses was thinking to himself, "Pharaoh doesn't like me. I'm not a good communicator and the children of Israel are not going to follow me out of Egypt." That's because Moses was thinking naturally about the supernatural plans of God.

God's supernatural plans will always succeed when you allow Him to push you forward into your calling and destiny. They will always succeed because they are contingent upon God's wisdom and sovereignty, not on your own wisdom, strength or abilities.

The full measure of the Spirit of God is always at work in ways, seen and unseen, to accomplish the supernatural plans and purposes of God. This is why the Bible says in Zechariah 4:6, "Not by might nor by power, but by my Spirit,› says the LORD Almighty." The Contemporary English Version puts it this way, "I am the LORD All-Powerful. So don›t depend on your own power or strength, but on my Spirit."

Exodus 3:12-15 says, "So God said, "I will certainly be with you. And this shall be a sign to you that I have sent you: When you have brought the people out of Egypt, you shall serve God on this mountain." Then Moses said to God, "Indeed, when I come to the children of Israel and say to them, 'The God of your fathers has sent me to you,' and they say to me, 'What is His name?' what shall I say to them?" And God said to Moses, "I am who I am." And He said, "Thus you shall say to the children of Israel, 'I Am has sent me to you.'"

I often laugh when I read this passage, but then I think of how many times we have very similar conversations with God. This can all be avoided if we simply agree with God as quickly as possible because, as we all know, God tends to have His way anyway. We simply need to have a genuine "yes!" in our spirit for whatever God calls us to. We need to live our lives in such a way that we always give God our yes, no matter what He may ask of us.

Exodus 4:10-11 says, "Then Moses said to the Lord, "O my Lord, I am not eloquent, neither before nor since You have spoken to Your servant; but I am slow of speech and slow of tongue." So the Lord said to him, "Who has made man's mouth? Or who makes the mute, the deaf, the seeing, or the blind? Have not I, the Lord?"

Once again, Moses is explaining all of his frailties and faults to God and then the Lord comes back and tells him, "I made you. And I know everything about you, Moses. You are the exact person that I'm going to use in this situation. Quit trying to talk you and Me both out of this." Moses felt so unworthy, but God knew that he was called.

God has placed a calling upon your life that is so far beyond your natural comprehension, you must rely on Him completely to fulfill it. God is looking to promote you to the very place that He has created you to occupy. But the devil, others and even yourself might have tried to convince you that you're not good enough or worthy enough, or that you don't belong there.

Sadly enough, many people will allow fear and insecurities to keep them back from walking in all that the Lord has for them, while others will answer the call of God and complete the calling that He has placed upon their lives. God wants us to surrender our entire lives to Him and to live in such a way that at the end of our lives we hear Jesus say, "Well done, good and faithful servant!"

Sometimes in life, you must look to Heaven, take a deep breath, and make the decision to fully receive all that God has for you. The choice is yours and no one else can make it for you. What will you choose?

Chapter 3:
The Heart of A King

In my wife's opinion, the greatest Disney movie of all time is Cinderella. Autumn says this is the classic fairytale story. The Bible has the male version of the Cinderella story. It is the story of King David. Here is the story of a young man who has been placed outside the comforts of the house to work a stricter schedule than his brothers. Now, we know they didn't share the same two parents and that surely plays a big part of why David was the one outside tending the sheep.

Without even knowing what God had planned for his life, David served his father and served him well. He had a good heart to help and seemed to be really adventurous. The Lord already had the perfect gift mix placed inside this young champion and had a plan setup to build his faith.

God teaches us all in different ways. Some may go to school while others may fight lions & bears. The path that God has for you is unique and will set you up to fulfill your destiny. As David was tending to his father's sheep, he learned how to play the harp and throw stones with his slingshot. The time David spent in the wilderness and in his cave season gave God plenty of time to train him into the perfect person for his future position as king!

When David was a young boy, he could have sat around and complained about his life. He could have grown bitter about how he was mistreated by his father. But, somewhere deep down inside, David knew there was more to life than his current situation. That was his destiny calling to him. His gifts and calling were pushing him to better himself while watching his father's sheep. Without yet knowing his ultimate position, David fine-tuned and learned different abilities. Learning these crafts helped David in his future.

In your life, you must always remember there is so much more coming your way than what you currently see. Keep learning and developing your gifts to further your calling. David went from being a shepherd to becoming a King. What will you become? Every time you feel unworthy, remember you are called. You may be tending to the sheep right now, but you are called.

The Lord spoke to the prophet, Samuel, to go to Jesse's house because God had chosen Israel's next king from among Jesse's sons. The Lord told Samuel, "Don't look at his appearance or physical stature." Jesse must have had some really good looking, well-groomed sons. But God has always been more focused on purity of heart than outward appearance.

God is always looking for someone to elevate into promising places of leadership and promotion. 2 Chronicles 16:9 says, "For the eyes of the Lord run to and fro throughout the whole earth, to show Himself strong on behalf of those whose heart is loyal to Him."

So Samuel went to the house of Jesse and told him one of his sons would be the next King. In great excitement, Jesse marched out his sons who all had great physical appearance and stature. He brought out his best-looking son, strongest son, smartest son, tallest son, most creative son, and so on, but God had not chosen any of them to be the future King of Israel.

Then Samuel said, "Are these all the sons you have?" Silence filled the room until Jesse said to one of his sons, "Go get David." When David came, Samuel poured the oil of the Lord over his head as David was anointed as King! David could have been mad and bitter, but instead he was full of gladness in his heart. David knew all the things he had been through up to that point in his life had led up to that particular moment in time.

The story of David is the male Biblical version of the Cinderella story. The one who could have easily felt unworthy was the one who was called to rule the Kingdom. You never know when your big day of promotion will come and you'll step into a complete manifestation of God's promises for your life. Who knows, it may be today! Someone go get the King, he is in the field! The oil of God always flows when the heart of man aligns with the purpose and calling of God.

We can never let the situation that we are currently in make us feel unworthy. When circumstances of life do not line up the way that you thought they would, just remember that you are called and keep moving forward. Sometimes life seems like running a 100-yard dash where you start off running with so much enthusiasm, but when you look up, there are 110 hurdles in front of you. The finish line is still the same distance as it was when you started. It didn't move. You just have to run a little bit harder and jump the hurdles to get to the finish line.

We must remember every day of our lives to keep pursuing God with a fiery burning passion for Him in our hearts, and also to keep moving forward in our God-given purpose. In every situation, you can either look at the good or the bad. In every person that you meet, you can look at the positive things about them or focus on their faults. This same principle applies to you. You can choose to be overwhelmed by negative thoughts about yourself or you can choose to focus on the positive. God wants you to believe in the you that He sees and continue to move forward in becoming the you He has called you to be.

Philippians 4:8 says, "Finally, brethren, whatever things are true, whatever things are noble, whatever things are just, whatever things are pure, whatever things are lovely, whatever things are of a good report, if there is any virtue and if there is anything praiseworthy, meditate on these things." Don't meditate on feelings of unworthiness. Instead throw your heart, mind and whole life into running hard after the destiny God has for you.

1 Corinthians 1:26 says, "For you see your calling, brethren, that not many wise according

to the flesh, not many mighty, not many noble, are called." Many people feel like they cannot respond fully to the call of God on their life because they are not wise, mighty or noble. In this passage, the word "wise" refers to the Greek philosophers. The word "mighty" refers to influential and political people. The word "noble" refers to those in the aristocratic upper class of society.

When I first felt the Lord call me to ministry, I looked at my life and named every single reason why God could not use me. But we must remember the word of God is stronger than the word of man. Without even knowing, I was speaking negative word curses over my life. But the powerful calling of God had already been spoken over my life. God had already placed it deep down into my spiritual DNA.

My friends, I can tell you I am walking 100% in the perfect will of God for my life and I have never been wise, noble or mighty by the world's standards. I had every reason to feel unworthy, but it did not matter to God because He had already called me. I have overcome every obstacle by the power of God. The areas I once considered myself weak in, are now the very things that God uses.

1 Corinthians 1:27-28 says, "But God has chosen the foolish things of the world to put to shame the wise, and God has chosen the weak things of the world to put to shame the things which are mighty; and the base things of the world and the things which are despised God has chosen, and the things which are not, to bring to nothing the things that are."

Whenever you are walking out the calling that God has upon your life, people may not always agree with you or the things that you are doing. When people completely surrender their lives to God, most people, including family and close friends, will ridicule them for their radical commitment.

This is because they think you will never be able to live a good enough life to accomplish the things you now know you're called to do.

They don't understand that it's not about rules and regulations but it is about a true, intimate relationship with Jesus. We are all worthy to walk in the calling that God has for us. After all, we didn't place the call upon ourselves. If God thinks we are worthy, that settles it!

Chapter 4:
Restoration

All throughout the Old Testament, it seems like the Philistines were always coming against the Israelites. The Philistines were trying to take the presence of God from the Israelites. The Philistines and surrounding nations must have understood that Israel's connection to God was their secret weapon because God always fought for them.

Whenever the enemy is fighting someone, he fights them the most for their personal private time with the Lord. Whenever someone does not spend time daily in their secret place, they are easily pulled away and are vulnerable to the enemy's schemes. If you lose the battle for your prayer life, you will lose your sensitivity to the Holy Spirit.

The Philistines constantly tried to capture the Ark of the Covenant which carried and represented the presence of God. That's why God's people must always remember to keep the presence of God the main priority in their lives. If you do not have the presence of God in your life and you fail to cultivate a close intimate relationship with Him daily, you are more likely to believe the lies of the enemy.

1 Samuel 13:19 says, "Now there was no blacksmith to be found throughout all the land of Israel, for the Philistines said, "Lest the Hebrews make swords or spears." The Philistines came and overpowered the Israelites and took away all of their weapons. The Philistines also removed all of the blacksmiths. Therefore, there were no ironworkers to make any swords or spears.

Now at this time the Philistine army was very fast and powerful. They seemed to have the assurance of victory for every single battle they entered. After overpowering the Israelites, taking their weapons and all of the people that made them, the Israelites felt very unworthy to ever even try to fight against them. I'm sure, by now, you know what the next sentence is going to be. "But the Israelites had a calling from God!"

During this time, the Israelites worked in the field to harvest their gardens and tend to their livestock. The Israelites had different tools they used in their farming. Some were to prod the oxen, some were to harvest the wheat. Basically, every tool they had in their hands to work with could be used as a weapon with a little imagination.

1 Samuel 13:20-22 says, "But all the Israelites went down and sharpened each man his plowshare, his mattock, his ax, and his sickle; and the charge for a sharpening was a pim [or about two-thirds of a shekel's weight] for the plowshares, the mattocks, the forks, and the axes, and to set the points of the goads. So, it came about, on the day of battle, that there was neither sword nor spear found in the hand of any of the people who were with Saul and Jonathan."

Sometimes, you may not have the tools you

think you need to overcome and advance in life, but you just need to identify and sharpen the tools that God has given you! You already have a weapon in your hand, it just needs to be sharpened so you can use it to overtake the enemy. Whatever you have in your hands is enough to bring you victory. God has placed enough inside of you to sustain you. You have enough information and knowledge to defeat every obstacle and get to the next level.

The Israelites had to go back and contend with the Philistines for their freedom and for the presence of God. There are times in your life when you have to fight for these two things. They go hand-in-hand. When you have the presence of God you will also have your freedom. Thankfully, we have the assurance that, as we fight the enemy's plans and tactics, God Himself fights with and for us. Isaiah 49:25 tells us, "But this is what the LORD says: "Yes, captives will be taken from warriors, and plunder retrieved from the fierce; I will contend with those who contend with you, and your children I will save."

Prepare yourself and align your heart to go after all the prophetic words God has spoken over your life. When you start getting yourself prepared and sharpening your God-given gifts and talents, the lies of unworthiness will start to fall off of you. You will regain your God-confidence and boldness to attempt and achieve great things with the Lord. Do whatever it takes. Fight whatever fight you must fight to regain the presence of God as the center point of your life.

Whenever God calls you to do something great for Him, everything that you possibly think could go wrong, usually will. Don't worry. All of these trials and tests will just make you stronger. Think about how David, playing with his slingshot while watching his father's sheep, ended up defeating a lion, a bear and eventually a giant. Think about how many hours David spent practicing with his slingshot. When he needed to use it to overcome the threat to his people, he was already well prepared.

I'm going to tell you one of my favorite non-biblical stories. This story is out of the diary of the great giant of the faith, John Wesley. This powerful man of God knew he was called to a region even though the people of the religious church establishment did not want him there. He knew He needed to preach the Word of the Lord that God had placed on his heart for his region, but it seemed that no minister or church would receive the Word of the Lord.

Whenever you're doing what God has called you to do, you will face opposition from people who do not want change. We must always remember that everywhere Jesus went, He brought change. Think about the lives of Jesus and Paul. Throughout their ministry, they were always welcomed by some and hated by others. Oftentimes, when people do not understand you or your calling, they will come against you. This is why we must always remember our calling and who we received it from.

The story goes that, as he prepared to go into this region, John Wesley's itinerary and heart were full and ready to bring change. But, on Sunday, May 5th, Wesley preached in St. Ann's and was asked to never come back. That same evening, Wesley preached at St. John's and the deacons said, "Get out and stay out!"

On Sunday, May 12th, Wesley preached in the morning at St. Jude's and was asked to never come back there either. That evening, Sunday, May12th, Wesley preached at St. George's and was kicked out again. On Sunday, May 19th, Wesley preached in the morning at St. Somebody else's church and the board got mad and said he wasn't welcome back. That same evening, Wesley preached on the street and was kicked off the street. On Sunday, May 26th, Wesley preached that morning in a meadow until they turned a bull out into the meeting in the meadow. On Sunday, June 2nd, Wesley preached at the edge of town, and was run completely out of town by angry townspeople. That night, Wesley preached in a pasture and 10,000 people showed up to hear him.

When the religious church establishment would not let John Wesley preach in their church or in their town, he didn't quit. He simply went right on outside the city limits and told everybody, "If you want more of God, come." 10,000 people, hungry for the true Word of God, wanted to hear what John Wesley had to say. They weren't hearing these types of messages from behind the pulpit in their churches. Their ministers did not carry the same passion and zeal for God. Therefore, the churches wanted him out of town, but he had a true call from God upon his life. God had a purpose for him to fulfill in that region.

Pat Schatzline says, "If someone believes in you, you win. If you believe in yourself, we all win." This is why so many friends of mine in ministry and I pour out our lives. We know that one God encounter in a service can change everything in someone's life. You never know who is sitting in an audience while you are ministering. One true encounter with God can mark them for life.

John 5:3-7 says, "In these lay a great multitude of sick people, blind, lame, paralyzed, waiting for the moving of the water. For an angel went down at a certain time into the pool and stirred up the water; then whoever stepped in first, after the stirring of the water, was made well of whatever disease he had. Now a certain man was there who had an infirmity 38 years. When Jesus saw him lying there, and knew that he already had been in that condition a long time, He said to him, "Do you want to be made well?" The sick man answered Him, "Sir, I have no man to put me into the pool when the water is stirred up; but while I am coming, another steps down before me."

Every time I read this passage, I think about how many people are just like this man laying by the pool. He realizes the fact that he needs help. He knew what his infirmity was and that he had been there for 38 years. He had allowed himself to become so used to his situation that he relied on plausible-sounding excuses to justify his condition.

So many people are just like this man because they are full of excuses but are not full of faith and hope. When Jesus asked the simple question, "Do you want to be made well?", the man replied with excuses. This man was probably so beat down by life and probably felt so unworthy to even be made well.

Many people would rather stay in that place of doubt, and mentally beat themselves up and feel unworthy than take the necessary steps to change. This man made so many excuses of why he could not be made whole. "Everyone cuts in front of me and no one will help me." Many people are just like this in life. They point fingers and blame everybody else to keep themselves a prisoner to their own toxic behavior, swimming in a sea of disbelief and self-pity.

Personally, if this was me, I would be sitting on the edge, halfway in the water and leaning over. So as soon as the water was troubled, I was going in. In life you will be around some people that are just "get it done!" people. These are the type of people the world calls type A personalities or "go getters!" They want to live their life to the absolute fullest, hit their mark and complete the call that God has on their life. This man at the pool was definitely not one of those people.

Now on the other hand, there is the determined lady in Matthew 9, the woman with the issue of blood. Matthew 9:20-22 says, "And suddenly, a woman who had a flow of blood for twelve years came from behind and touched the hem of His garment. For she said to herself, "If only I may touch His garment, I shall be made well." But Jesus turned around, and when He saw her He said, "Be of good cheer, daughter; your faith has made you well." And the woman was made well from that hour."

In those days, if you had a condition like hers you were considered dirty and unclean. Therefore, you had to live outside the gate of the city that was fortified by walls. So, the first thing she had to do to get to Jesus was to break into the city, go through the gates of the town and past the guards to even get inside. She then found Jesus, which was easy because there was a huge crowd around Him. But then she had to fight through the whole crowd and the 12 disciples, just to touch the hem of His garment.

Now having a flow of blood for this many years means that she was probably a very weak, little woman. But nothing was going to stop her from getting her healing. She was determined because she knew she had a lot of life left to live, and she wanted to be healed so she could complete the call that God had on her life.

Jeremiah 18:1-4 says, "The word which came to Jeremiah from the Lord, saying: "Arise and go down to the potter's house, and there I will cause you to hear My words." Then I went down to the potter's house, and there he was, making something at the wheel. And the vessel that he made of clay was marred in the hand of the potter; so he made it again into another vessel, as it seemed good to the potter to make."

There is such an important lesson to learn from this passage. Whenever the potter was making the vessel, if it became marred, blemished or looked unworthy in any way, it wasn't thrown away! It was simply placed back on the wheel, crushed or pressed down to start again. This continued until the vessel took the shape the potter intended. Some of you need to get back on the wheel and allow the Potter to start working on you again.

Our God is a restoring God. God restores you because He loves you and He wants to use you. God doesn't see you as unworthy. He recognizes the call that He placed upon you. Some of you just simply need to let the Potter place His hands back on you and have full control of your destiny.

If you realized fully the awesome life that God has planned for you, you would spend more time with Him in prayer allowing Him to equip you for your next level assignment. Every new season of our life is supposed to get better with the Lord as we live out the calling He has placed upon us. If you could only see what God has planned for you in the future, you would prepare yourself at a greater level.

Chapter 5:
Lose the Labels

There are so many words that people use to identify themselves. Sometimes people will even use certain words to label other people, even though their labels don't match what God has said about that person. Never allow someone to label you or you to label yourself with some name, title, or condition that does not align with your God-given identity. Usually, if you can remove the prefix from these words, you will see the actual truth that should be spoken over your life.

The first word I want to address today is the word unworthy. The word "unworthy" means not acceptable, especially by someone else with a good reputation or social position. This word means that you are rejected and not accepted by a certain person or group of people. The definition talks about a good reputation or social position. The person with the best reputation is Jesus and the highest social position is God. So, this word implies that you should not be able to associate with them or ever be worthy enough to carry out your calling.

Now, let's remove the prefix, "un". What is left implies that you *are* worthy and accepted by God. You are worthy to carry out all the purposes and plans that He has for your life. Understand this, just like the prefix, people will try to attach a label to you that does not belong to you to try to weigh you down. The presence or absence of the prefix in this word completely changes its meaning and the way that we look at it. The word "worthy" means possessing qualities or abilities that merit recognition.

God has given you special gifts and your calling and has placed His approval upon you, therefore, you *can* do all that He has called you to do. You are worthy to have a close personal relationship with the Lord. The enemy will try to add a prefix to your life to make you look unworthy in the eyes of others. He may even try to make you feel unworthy in your own eyes. But, my friends, you are always worthy in the eyes of God.

So many feel so undeserving to do what the Lord has called them to do. They feel undeserving to have a close walk with the Lord and struggle with a sense of illegitimacy. The word "undeserving" means not deserving, or not worthy of anything positive, especially help or praise. Once again, if you remove the prefix from this word, you will understand that you deserve to be all that God said you could be and do. You should by no means ever feel ineligible or illegitimate again. The word ineligible means legally or officially unable to be considered for a position or benefit.

Sometimes we believe word curses that have been spoken over our lives so strongly that it makes us feel ineligible to walk in the blessings and benefits God has specially appointed for our lives. I'm here to tell you that you have legal and official rights to be considered for every position that God has called you to. I said, by the grace and power of God, you are eligible!

Many people feel like they are unqualified to do what God has called them to do. The word "unqualified" means not officially recognized as a practitioner of a particular profession or activity. When the Lord speaks a profound word of destiny to your heart, the enemy will come in and try to make you feel unqualified. But, you must always remember that God is not going to call you to something easy that could be accomplished in your own strength. He will call you to things that require you to fully and completely rely on Him. You are qualified, my friend, to go live your God-given dreams. What are you waiting for? Go forth in Jesus name!

There are not many things in this world that I dislike more than insecurity. The word "insecurity" means uncertainty or anxiety about oneself or lack of confidence. This is one of the biggest issues in the church today.

So many people are walking around with hidden gifts and talents but because they are so insecure, they feel as though they could never use them.

Many people lack confidence and are afraid they are going to mess up. When you realize the love of the Father, and how much He truly cares about you, every bit of insecurity will fade away. When you choose to believe and rest in the truth of God's love, you will be secure in your relationship with the Lord and in your calling. You will have the confidence and boldness to go after the promises God has made to you and the words He has spoken over your life. Insecurity must go out of your life in the name of Jesus!

The Bible says that King David encouraged himself in the Lord daily. 1 Samuel 30:6 tells us that King David was under a lot of stress, opposition and pressure from many. But, King David encouraged himself in the Lord. People were even speaking about stoning David. Nevertheless, he encouraged himself daily. Each and every morning, I look at myself in the mirror and I speak life over myself. I recite the different prophetic words that have been spoken over my life. As I stare at myself in the mirror, I quote the word of God to myself and speak life and blessing over my family, friends and ministries.

Sadly enough, many people in the church today feel that they are unfit to serve in the Kingdom of God. The word "unfit" means not of the necessary quality or standard to meet a particular purpose. I love the stories of Jeremiah and Moses in the Bible when they tried to convince God that they were unfit to carry out the plans He had for them. Listen, you are not just fit, you are well-fitted for the things the Lord has planned for you. Just like when a lady gets a custom-made dress, or a man gets a tailor-made suit. You are perfectly fitted for the calling and plan that God has for you.

Many believe they are unsuitable to fill a position in the Kingdom of God. That is a lie from the very pit of Hell. The word "unsuitable" means not fitting or appropriate. Once again, you have to believe the truth that you are exactly who the Lord wants to use. Yes, you are the one that God is about to use in the days ahead because you are suitable to do the work of the Lord. Don't settle in life because you think you don't measure up. Don't think you are unsuitable to go after the dreams that are hidden inside of you. You are the perfect fit to fulfill the call God has placed on your life.

In the times ahead, the Church is going to walk in some glorious days. Church as usual will not cut it anymore, but revival and awakening will be our portion. We are going to enter into a season of moral reformation, but it must first start in the hearts of those who may feel unworthy but know they are called.

The word "inappropriate" means not suitable or proper in the circumstances. The enemy wants you to believe you are inappropriate for your part in God's great plan. But the reality is that, in the current state the world finds itself in, you are completely appropriate. In fact, God has made you uniquely suited to the role He has appointed for you in His Kingdom. This is your time to go full throttle after God and the things He has for you. The world is waiting for you to step up and take your appropriate place in the Kingdom of God!

The word "improper" means not in accordance with accepted rules or standards. One of the biggest lies and tricks of the enemy is to try to get people to feel like they do not measure up to what God has spoken over them or the potential He has placed on the inside of them. The devil tries to make believers feel like there is a certain standard we must live, and then if we fall short, he wants to make us feel as though we are the improper choice to accomplish great things for God.

This is where religion comes in. It makes people desperately try to look right in the eyes of others and appear as though they have it all together to fit a certain standard. In truth, God isn't after rule followers. Rather, He wants us to have an authentic, intimate relationship with Him.

My friend, you are properly placed by God Himself. The Lord has properly placed the right gift mix inside of you to accomplish the call He has for you. So, go after everything He's called you to! You are well-equipped for the days and the journey ahead. Let God-adventures be your portion and lose the labels others have placed on you!

Chapter 6:
They're Just Beans

I believe one of the saddest stories in the Bible is the story of Jacob and Esau. This story is about one brother wanting the birthright of another one. Jacob wanted so badly to have his brother's blessing that he was willing to charge him for something he should have given freely. This is also a story about a man who did not fully grasp the reality of all that God and his father had stored up for him. When we do not understand the value of our birthright in Jesus Christ, we too will be tempted to trade everything God has for us for next to nothing.

Genesis 25:29-34 says, "Now Jacob cooked a stew; and Esau came in from the field, and he was weary. And Esau said to Jacob, "Please feed me with that same red stew, for I am weary." Therefore, his name was called Edom. But Jacob said, "Sell me your birthright as of this day." And Esau said, "Look, I am about to die; so what is this birthright to me?" Then Jacob said, "Swear to me as of this day." So he swore to him, and sold his birthright to Jacob. And Jacob gave Esau bread and stew of lentils; then he ate and drank, arose, and went his way. Thus Esau despised his birthright."

The importance of the birthright in this story is this: the oldest son did not just get the best and largest sections of his father's land, he was also the ruler over the whole family after his father passed. Let's say that there were four sons, instead of each son getting 25% of the land, the oldest son would get 40%, while the other three brothers would get 20%. Now the oldest brother would also get to pick his portion first, then the other brothers would get the leftovers. So, when Esau gave away his birthright, he gave away a huge portion of land, and the right to be the ruler and high priest over the family. He gave all of this away for a bowl of lentil soup! In essence, he gave his spiritual and geographical inheritance and legacy away for something without great or lasting value.

So many times, people give away precious things for something that may please the flesh for a short season. Seriously, we are talking about a bowl of lentils here. It wasn't even pinto beans or black beans, but it was a bowl of lentils. You may read the story and say, "How in the world could you give away your calling and that position for something so small?" Well, people do it all the time.

People give away their character, integrity, marriages, positions and companies all the time for temporary pleasures of the flesh. So many people give the things God has planned for them up for something as simple as a bowl of lentil soup. How many lives has pornography ruined? How many times has alcohol destroyed families? Gambling addictions have caused families to lose everything. When we understand how much

God loves us, and how much He has in store for us and wants to give us even now, we won't just look different, we will become different.

When you read Hebrews 12, the story makes a lot of sense. Hebrews 12:15-16 says, "Looking carefully lest anyone fall short of the grace of God; lest any root of bitterness springing up cause trouble, and by this many become defiled; lest there be any fornicator or profane person like Esau, who for one morsel of food sold his birthright." You see, Esau was known as a fornicator, someone who wasn't walking uprightly before the Lord. When you're not walking close to God, living a daily life of private devotion, you will be easily swayed by the deceiver.

Just like Esau, many people give away the things God has for them for one simple moment of pleasure or a self-gratifying, fleshly encounter. In Jacob and Esau's father's house, there were many cooks and servants. If Esau could have waited just a little bit longer, he could have walked in, had anything he wanted prepared for him to eat, and kept his birthright! Many people will give away the trust of others, and things they've worked for, for one night on the town or one moment of pleasure. Sadly, afterwards, they live a lifetime full of regret.

God is raising up a remnant who will keep the fire of God burning fervently in their heart and in their eyes to move forward in advancing the Kingdom of God. 1 Peter 3:15, in the New Heart English Bible, says, "But sanctify in your hearts Christ as Lord; and always be ready to give an answer to everyone who asks you a reason concerning the hope that is in you, yet with humility and fear." Fear here means having a reverential awe of God and walking in Christlike meekness. God is raising up a people who will so honor Christ in their hearts and lives that there is absolutely no room for any competing idols or fleshly desires.

One day as I was reading this story, I yelled, "Esau, they're just beans!" When you get a heavenly perspective of the destiny that God has for you, you will not give in to fleshly temptations. You will rise above them and receive God's abundant grace to be continuously filled with His Spirit as a true man or woman of valor for the Lord!

Another one of my favorite stories in the Bible is the one about Shammah who was one of King David's mighty men. This is a man that got a command and stayed with it no matter what came against him. 2 Samuel 23:8-12 says, "These are the names of the mighty men whom David had: And after him was Shammah the son of Agee the Hararite. The Philistines had gathered together into a troop where there was a piece of ground full of lentils. So the people fled from the Philistines. But he stationed himself in the middle of the field, defended it, and killed the Philistines. So the Lord brought about a great victory."

Once again, we're talking about lentils. Shammah got the command from King David, "Get some men together and guard the field of lentils." So Shammah went out and got the roughest and toughest warriors he could find to form an army. The Bible says that when the troop of Philistines started running towards the field, all of the other Israelite soldiers took off running in fear, but Shammah stayed.

The men who were running from the fight probably yelled, "Come on, let's get out of here. They're just beans!" But, in this instance, these lentils and the land they were on was the very thing King David told them to fight for. If they lost the fight that day, they would have to come back and try to regain the ground another day. The one who stayed was the one who was given the command.

Those lentils were used for food and also to trade for livestock and clothing. Shammah saw the value in the land and the lentils at a greater capacity than the ones that fled. Shammah realized that he was fighting for his family, his friends and his region. While some people just thought it was a simple field of lentils, he understood that defending that field was his calling and that doing so was also evidence of his faithfulness to the command of the king.

Notice that the one who received the calling and command stayed, while the others fled. Sometimes you are going to have to fight for something even if you have to stand alone. Many times, everybody beside you will leave. But remember, if you are the one called, you will stay. Never let uncommitted people pull you away from the calling God has spoken over you. Never let someone make you change your geographical location when the Lord has placed you somewhere.

After this epic battle was over, the Bible says God got a great victory. The reason it doesn't say Shammah got the victory, is because one man could not defeat a full troop of Philistines unless God gave him the strength. You will have the strength to stand firm and faithful in the field God has placed you in and you too will have a great victory!

Shammah found something to stand for. He found something worth dying for. He found a cause greater than himself. When you find your calling, you will completely throw your life into it. You are worthy to stand in the field to which you've been called. You are worthy to fight the battles that are before you. God will give you the strength and the victory in the days ahead.

The reason the enemy fights people so hard with feelings of unworthiness is because he knows if people are always worried about themselves, they will never be able to help anybody else. When we're fighting in spiritual warfare, we're not just fighting for ourselves. We are fighting for everybody around us and those connected by God to us.

Whenever people are going through seasons where they are battling feelings of unworthiness, I tell them there's a three-step process to get past that: read, fast and pray. When you dive into the word of God and the Bible comes alive to you, you cannot help but feel excited about what God has in store for you!

The Bible has over 7,000 promises that will

shake you to your core. One of my favorites is Psalms 119:9-11 which says, 'How can a young man cleanse his way? By taking heed according to Your word. With my whole heart I have sought You; Oh, let me not wander from Your commandments! Your word have I hidden in my heart, That I might not sin against You."

When you hide the written Word and the prophetic Word of God in your heart, nothing can ever make you feel unworthy to do all that your heavenly Father has called you to do. I believe you have greatness on the inside of you or you wouldn't have even bought this book. Never let anybody or any situation make you feel unworthy when God has already called you to do great things. If you keep a forever "Yes!" in your spirit toward the Lord, He will forever keep opening doors for you! Get ready to accomplish great things for the Kingdom of God. You are called and you are worthy!

About The Author

Joe Joe Dawson is the founder and Apostle of ROAR Apostolic Network and Roar Church Texarkana. Joe Joe is married to the love of his life, Autumn Dawson. They have three children Malachi, Judah and Ezra. The Dawson's teach a lifestyle of revival and awakening. Their desire is to see every believer fulfill their God-given destiny and live life to the fullest in God. Joe Joe is the author of such books as The 40 P's of the Apostolic, Moving Forward and Kingdom Mindset.

CHECK OUT THE OTHER BOOKS FROM JOE JOE DAWSON

Moving Forward
40 P's Of The Apostolic
Kingdom Mindset
Destiny Dimensions: A 60 Day Devotional
Living Your God Sized Dream
Recipe For Revival

**FOR MORE INFORMATION VISIT,
JOEJOEDAWSON.NET**

CONNECT WITH US
SUBSCRIBE + FOLLOW

JOE JOE DAWSON
FACEBOOK

@JOE_JOE_DAWSONTXK
INSTAGRAM

@PASTORJOEDAWSON
TWITTER

JOE JOE DAWSON
YOUTUBE

@JOEJOEDAWSON
PERISCOPE

JOEJOEDAWSON.NET
WEBSITE

LIVING OUR *best* LIFE

MARRIAGE · FAMILY · LIFESTYLE

LIVINGOURBESTLIFE.NET

Roar U is the online learning center of Joe Joe Dawson Ministries. We want to see you fully equipped in your individual callings, gifts, dreams, purpose & destiny. Our desire is to provide valuable resources to propel you forward. Roar U continues to grow and expand with new topics, articles and videos.

Check it out at roaru.tv

Roar Apostolic Network is a network of believers who are contending for revival and awakening. Our heart is to help train and equip every person and ministry that comes into alignment with us. We are called to walk in the fullness of God's authority and power while abiding in the Father's love. Our calling is to help others reach their God-given dreams and destiny. This network is built for a church, ministry, pastor, business person, intercessor, believer, etc. ROAR stands for Revival, Outpouring, Awakening, and Reformation.

For more information, visit roarapostolicnetwork.com

Roar Church is an Apostolic community of believers passionate about the Kingdom of God in Texarkana, Texas. It was founded in 2017 by Apostle Joe Joe & Autumn Dawson. Roar Church is a gathering of believers seeking the presence and power of God together. It is our desire for revival, outpouring, awakening and reformation to transform our region and see the Kingdom of God manifested in the earth.

For more information, visit roarchurchtexarkana.com

CPSIA information can be obtained
at www.ICGtesting.com
Printed in the USA
BVHW041332240222
630007BV00013B/783